Maple Syrup

Over 75 Farm Fresh Recipes

D1302146

Hatherleigh Press is committed to preserving and protecting the natural resources of the Earth. Environmentally responsible and sustainable practices are embraced within the company's mission statement.

Hatherleigh Press is a member of the Publishers Earth Alliance, committed to preserving and protecting the natural resources of the planet while developing a sustainable business model for the book publishing industry.

This book was edited and designed in the village of Hobart, New York. Hobart is a community that has embraced books and publishing as a component of its livelihood. There are several unique bookstores in the village. For more information, please visit www.hobartbookvillage.com.

www.hatherleighpress.com

DISCLAIMER
This book offers general cooking and eating suggestions for educational purposes only.
In no case should it be a substitute nor replace a healthcare professional. Consult your healthcare professional to determine which foods are safe for you and to establish the right diet for your personal nutritional needs.

Library of Congress Cataloging-in-Publication Data is available upon request.
ISBN: 978-1-57826-369-1

All Hatherleigh Press titles are available for bulk purchase, special promotions, and premiums. For information about reselling and special purchase opportunities, please call 1-800-528-2550 and ask for the Special Sales Manager.

Cover Design by Nick Macagnone
Photography by Catarina Astrom
Interior Design by Nick Macagnone
10 9 8 7 6 5 4 3 2 1

hatherleigh
Improve your life. Change your world.

Acknowledgments

Hatherleigh Press would like to extend a special thank you to Jo Brielyn—without your hard work and creativity this book would not have been possible.

Table of Contents

All About Maple Syrup

The process of creating maple syrup, also called sugaring, has been around since Native Americans developed a technique of cutting into maple trees and collecting the sap in crude vessels. They would then place heated stones in the containers filled with the sweet, watery substance to evaporate the water, thus producing maple syrup. The syrup was used for both medicine and food. The Native Americans later taught these methods to early settlers, who also noticed the many benefits of the syrup and used their knowledge and tools to improve on the processes of tapping trees and boiling the sap over a fire.

To convert recipes and substitute maple syrup for granulated white sugar or brown sugar, follow this simple rule:

For every 1 cup of sugar, use ¾ to 1 cup maple syrup, depending on the desired level of sweetness. Be sure to slightly reduce another liquid in the recipe to avoid the end product becoming too runny.

Although sugaring methods have changed with time and technology, the basic premise is still the same. Maple syrup is produced by boiling down the sap found in maple trees until almost all of the water has evaporated. As the water leaves the liquid, it becomes darker and sweeter. Tree sap that starts with a sugar content of about 2% slowly turns into maple syrup that is roughly 65% sugar, making it an excellent natural sweetener. In fact, maple syrup is a less refined sugar that may be substituted in most recipes that require white or brown sugar.

In addition to being a natural sweetener, maple syrup also contains minerals and antioxidants that improve health and strengthen the immune system. It has significant amounts of calcium, manganese, and potassium, and small amounts of iron, zinc, phosphorous, and B vitamins. Maple syrup is 68% carbohydrates, as compared to 100% in most other syrups, and is low in sodium.

Maple products also contain antioxidants known to have anti-cancer, anti-bacterial, and anti-diabetic properties.

Where is Maple Syrup Produced?

Maple syrup is produced only in North American regions where sugar maples are found—the northeastern United States and eastern Canada. In 2010, there were 1.96 million gallons of maple syrup produced in the United States alone. America's maple producers are located in the northeastern states of Vermont, New York, Maine, Wisconsin, New Hampshire, Michigan, Ohio, Pennsylvania, Massachusetts, and Connecticut.

There are four U.S. grades of maple syrup (although grading standards vary slightly from state to state). Maple syrup grades are dependent on the time of season in which the syrup is collected and the trees being tapped. One grade of maple syrup is not necessarily better than another. It is a matter of personal preference.

Here are the four grades of maple syrup determined by the United States Department of Agriculture (USDA):

Grade A Light Amber – This syrup is very light and mild tasting. It usually is made from sap collected early in the season when the weather is colder and is generally considered the highest grade. Grade A Light Amber is best used for making candy, maple sugar, and maple cream.

Grade A Medium Amber – Syrup in this grade is slightly darker and has more maple flavor. It generally comes from sap collected midseason. Grade A Medium Amber is the most popular grade for table syrup.

Grade A Dark Amber – This maple syrup is darker and has a much more robust maple flavor. It is usually made later in the season and is excellent for table syrup and general use.

Grade B – Maple syrup in this grade is the darkest and strongest-tasting of all the grades. Some people use it as table syrup, but due to its strong maple and caramel flavors, Grade B syrup is often used for cooking, baking and flavoring.

Did you know?

- It takes 40 to 50 gallons of sap to make 1 gallon of maple syrup.
- Maple syrup is 100% fat free!
- The season for tapping trees only lasts for 8-10 weeks and runs from February until early April.
- Regardless of the varying degrees of flavor and color, all grades of syrup are processed in the same manner and have the same consistency.
- Tapping a maple tree does no permanent damage to it.
- You can store maple syrup in the freezer to retain flavor and quality, and it will not freeze.

Breakfast

Maple Granola

(Courtesy of the New York State Maple Producers Association, www.nysmaple.com)

Ingredients:

3 cups old-fashioned rolled oats
½ cup sliced almonds
½ cup roasted cashews
½ cup roasted sesame seeds
½ cup roasted sunflower seeds
¼ cup unsalted butter
½ cup pure Grade B maple syrup
½ cup vegetable oil
½ teaspoon vanilla extract
¼ cup granulated pure maple sugar
1 cup raisins or dried cranberries

Directions:

Preheat oven to 325°F. In a large bowl, combine the oats, almonds, cashews, sesame seeds, and sunflower seeds.

In a small saucepan, combine the butter, maple syrup, oil, vanilla, and maple sugar. Cook over medium heat for 5 minutes. Pour over the dry mixture and stir until well blended. Spread the mixture out on a baking sheet in an even layer. Bake, stirring occasionally, for about 30 minutes or until golden. Remove from the oven and let cool. Stir in the raisins or cranberries. Store in an airtight container at room temperature for up to 2 weeks.

Marylee's Stuffed French Toast
(Courtesy of Shaver-Hill Farm, www.shaverhillfarm.com)

Ingredients:

8 slices bread

1 (8 oz.) package cream cheese

12 eggs

2 cups milk

½ cup pure maple syrup

Directions:

Cube bread and put half in a 9 x12-inch pan. Cube cream cheese and place on top of the bread, then add remaining bread. Beat eggs together with milk and maple syrup, then pour over cream cheese and bread. Cover with plastic wrap and refrigerate over-night.

Bake at 375°F for 45 minutes. Serve with maple syrup.

French Toast

Ingredients:

2 eggs
1 cup milk
1 teaspoon sugar
1 teaspoon cinnamon (optional)
1 pinch salt
4-6 slices stale bread

Directions:

Beat eggs. Add milk, sugar, cinnamon (optional), and salt to mixture, and blend well. Dip slices of stale bread in the egg and milk mixture. Fry in a lightly greased pan or griddle. Serve with pure maple syrup.

Maple Sour Cream Muffins

(Courtesy of the New York State Maple Producers Association,
www.nysmaple.com)

Ingredients:

1¾ cups flour
1 teaspoon baking soda
2 teaspoons baking powder
½ teaspoon salt
½ cup butter
1¾ cups pure maple syrup
1 cup sour cream
1 egg
½ cup chopped pecans
Pure maple cream (optional)

Directions:

Preheat oven to 400°F. Grease a 16-cavity standard muffin pan.
Stir together all dry ingredients (except pecans) and set aside.
In another bowl, cream butter. Add maple syrup, sour cream,
and egg. Stir in pecans. Add the dry ingredients and stir until
blended. Spoon batter in pan about ⅔ full. Bake 15-17 minutes.
Cool and remove from pan. Drizzle with maple cream if desired.

Pancakes

Ingredients:
1 teaspoon baking powder
2 cups flour
4 eggs
1 teaspoon salt
2 cups milk

Directions:
Blend baking powder and flour in a small bowl. Beat the whites and yolks of eggs separately. Add the egg yolks, salt, egg whites, and half of the milk in a mixing bowl. Gradually add the flour mixture and the remainder of milk, alternating between the two until the batter is of the desired consistency. Grease the bottom of a hot frying pan, pour in a large ladleful of batter, and fry quickly. Serve with pure maple syrup.

Maple Sticky Buns

(Courtesy of the New York State Maple Producers Association,
www.nysmaple.com)

Ingredients:

Dough

1⅛ cups water
¼ cup pure granulated maple sugar
1½ teaspoons salt
8 tablespoons butter
½ cup barley flour
2⅔ cups bread flour
½ cup dry milk
2½ teaspoons yeast

Filling

6 tablespoons butter, softened
1½ cups pure granulated maple sugar
4 teaspoons cinnamon

Topping

6 tablespoons melted butter
½ cup pure maple syrup
1 teaspoon cinnamon

Directions:

Dough

Place room temperature water in mixing bowl, then add remaining ingredients in order listed. Yeast should be added last in an indentation in the dry ingredients. Knead for approximately 5 minutes. When dough is finished, place on lightly floured board. Punch dough down and shape into an 8-inch wide rectangle (20 inches long).

Filling

Cream together the softened butter, maple sugar, and cinnamon to form a paste. Spread the filling evenly on the dough, and then roll.

Topping

Melt butter in a 9 x 13-inch baking pan. Mix with the syrup and cinnamon. Let stand until ready to put dough in the pan.

Cut the dough roll into 16 slices and place on the syrup mixture in the baking pan. Cover and let rise about 45 minutes. Preheat oven to 375°F. Bake for 20-25 minutes. Invert to serve.

Maple Oatmeal Bread

(Courtesy of the New York State Maple Producers Association,
www.nysmaple.com)

Ingredients:
1 cup water, room temperature
½ cup regular rolled oats
1 tablespoon butter
2 tablespoons pure maple syrup
1 teaspoon salt
½ cup whole wheat flour
2 cups bread flour
1¼ tablespoons gluten
1¼ teaspoons yeast

Directions:
Pour the room temperature water into a bowl. Add oats and let
stand 20 minutes, if possible, before adding remaining ingredients in order listed. Bake in bread pan at 375°F for 28-30
minutes.

Variation: Use another tablespoon of maple syrup for more
maple taste—the bread will also brown more.

Banana Smoothie

(Courtesy of Chef Nancy Berkoff, R.D., The Vegetarian Resource
Group Food Service Update, www.vrg.org)

Ingredients:

1 (6 oz.) container fruited soy yogurt (any flavor)
3 tablespoons soft silken tofu
1 medium ripe banana (approximately ½ cup sliced)
½ cup rice milk or fruit juice
1 tablespoon pure maple syrup

Directions:

Combine all ingredients in a blender and blend well. You can add
more juice or more solid ingredients, depending on the texture
you need.

Yields 1 large serving.

Soups & Salads

Maple and Parsnip Soup

(Courtesy of the New York State Maple Producers Association,
www.nysmaple.com)

Ingredients:

3 pounds parsnips, peeled and sliced ¼-inch thick
1 large white onion, peeled and sliced ¼-inch thick
8 cups water
1 cup pure maple syrup
1 large bay leaf
1 cup heavy cream
Salt and white pepper to taste

Directions:

Lightly brown parsnips and onions with vegetable oil in sauce pan, season lightly with salt and white pepper. Add water, maple syrup, bay leaf, and cover. Keep flame low and simmer until tender. Pull out bay leaf and puree all remaining ingredients in a food processor until smooth. Pour ingredients back into pot, add heavy cream, and reheat, being careful not to boil. Season to taste with salt and white pepper. Drizzle with maple syrup and serve warm with crusty bread.

Roasted Acorn Squash and Apple Soup

(Courtesy of the New York State Maple Producers Association,
www.nysmaple.com)

Ingredients:

1 medium acorn squash,
quartered, seeds removed
(see note below)
1 cup onions, peeled and diced
1 cup carrots, peeled and diced
1 cup celery, diced
3 apples (such as Cortland
or McIntosh), peeled, cored
and diced small
3 cloves garlic, minced
2 cups sherry wine

1 quart low-sodium chicken
stock or chicken broth
1 cup heavy cream
1 cup pure maple syrup
Cider vinegar, to taste
Pure maple sugar, for garnish
Oil, as needed
Salt and pepper to taste

Directions:

Place the acorn squash quarters on an oiled sheet tray, drizzle squash
with oil and sprinkle with salt and pepper. Cover the entire tray with
foil and bake in a 425°F oven for about 30 minutes or until starting
to turn tender. Remove foil and bake an additional 30 minutes or until
fork tender. Remove from oven. When cool enough to handle, scoop out
flesh from squash skin. Discard skins. Heat a skillet over high heat until
hot. Add enough oil to lightly coat the bottom of the pan and sauté the
onions, carrots and celery until onions are translucent and caramelized.
Add the apples and garlic and sauté 1-2 minutes more. Add the sherry
wine and bring to a boil. Reduce by half. Add stock and bring to a boil.
Let mixture simmer until apples and carrots are very tender, about 20
minutes. Add roasted squash. Finish with heavy cream, maple syrup,
salt and pepper to taste. For flavor enhancement, add a splash of cider
vinegar to the soup and stir well. Puree the soup with a stick blender,
regular blender, or in a high-quality food processor until very smooth.
Ladle soup into baked warm bowls and sprinkle with maple sugar before
serving.

Note: If desired, wash the acorn squash seeds under cold water, sprinkle
with salt, then spread on a sheet tray and roast in a 275°F oven until
dried and crispy, about 40-50 minutes. Serve atop soup with maple
sugar.

Walnut and Wild Rice Salad

(Courtesy of Chef Nancy Berkoff, R.D., "Food Service Update",
The Vegetarian Resource Group, www.vrg.org)

Ingredients:

Salad:

2 cups uncooked wild rice
1 cup chopped dark raisins
1 cup chopped toasted walnuts
½ cup chopped toasted cashews
½ cup chopped green onion
2 ounces chopped celery
1 ounce chopped onion

Dressing:

2 ounces red wine vinegar
2 tablespoons lemon juice
2 tablespoons fresh or frozen, thawed raspberries
2 cloves minced garlic
1 teaspoon pure maple syrup
¼ cup olive oil

Directions:

Salad:

Combine rice and 6 cups water in a pot. Bring to a fast boil.
Reduce heat, cover, and allow to simmer until the rice is tender,
about 40 minutes. Drain and allow to cool. Combine cooled rice
with raisins, walnuts, cashews, green onion, celery, and onion in
a bowl.

Dressing:

Pour vinegar, lemon juice, raspberries, garlic, and maple syrup
into a blender or food processor canister. With blender or food
processor on low, slowly pour in oil. Allow to combine. Toss
dressing with rice. Serve at room temperature or chilled.

Maple Fruit Salad

(Courtesy of the New York State Maple Producers Association,
www.nysmaple.com)

Ingredients:

⅓ cup heavy whipping cream
½ cup pure maple syrup
⅔ cup low-fat vanilla yogurt
4 cups strawberries, sliced
2 cups pineapple chunks
1½ cups blueberries
1 cup cantaloupe chunks
¼ cup pine nuts (optional)
Pinch cinnamon

Directions:

Whisk cream until thickened, then whisk in maple syrup until
mixed. Add yogurt and cinnamon. Pour over mixed fruit and
add pine nuts if desired.

Maple Blender French Dressing

(Courtesy of the New York State Maple Producers Association,
www.nysmaple.com)

Ingredients:

1 cup ketchup
½ cup pure maple syrup
1 teaspoon salt
¾ cup salad oil (such as safflower, olive, canola, or sunflower)
¼ teaspoon pepper
½ teaspoon dry mustard
½ teaspoon powdered ginger

Directions:

Place all ingredients in blender, cover, and blend on high speed
for 20 seconds. Makes 2 cups.

Maple Vinaigrette Salad Dressing
(Courtesy of the New York State Maple Producers Association,
www.nysmaple.com)

Ingredients:
½ cup pure granulated maple sugar
½ cup white vinegar
½ cup canola oil
½ teaspoon paprika
¼ teaspoon garlic powder
½ teaspoon dry mustard
¼ teaspoon pepper
½ teaspoon Mrs. Dash® Table Blend Seasoning
½ teaspoon Worcestershire sauce

Directions:
Combine all ingredients in a bottle that will seal tightly. Shake vigorously prior to use. Store in refrigerator.

Note: This salad dressing is almost entirely salt-free! There is a negligible amount of salt in the Worcestershire sauce.

Maple and Balsamic Vinegar Dressing

(Courtesy of the Massachusetts Maple Producers Association,
www.massmaple.org)

Ingredients:

1 teaspoon dry mustard
1 teaspoon cilantro
3 tablespoons balsamic vinegar
2 tablespoons pure maple syrup
1 tablespoon lime juice
1 clove garlic, minced
1 cup extra-virgin olive oil
Salt and pepper to taste

Directions:

Mix together the first six ingredients. Whisk in oil until dressing
is emulsified. Add salt and pepper to taste. Refrigerate to store
for several weeks.

Poppy Seed Maple Syrup Salad Dressing

(Courtesy of the New York State Maple Producers Association,
www.nysmaple.com)

Ingredients:

4 tablespoons pure maple syrup
½ cup vegetable oil
¼ cup orange juice (or to taste)
1½ teaspoons poppy seeds
Salt and pepper to taste

Directions:

In a jar with a tight lid, combine all ingredients and shake well.

Note: For a nice early summer salad, serve with green leaf lettuce, strawberry slices (or red grape halves), and green onion slices.

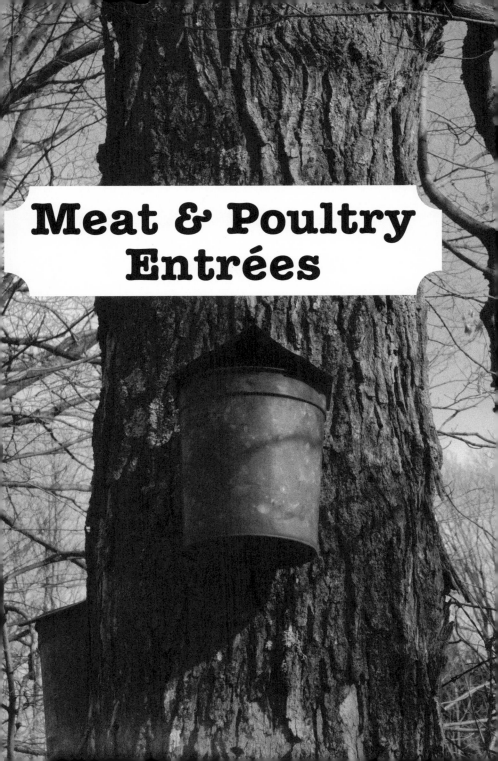

Meat & Poultry Entrées

Maple Chicken

(Courtesy of Shaver-Hill Farm, www.shaverhillfarm.com)

Ingredients:
1 (2½-3 lb.) chicken
¼ cup melted butter
½ cup pure maple syrup
½ teaspoon grated lemon rind
½ teaspoon salt
¼ cup chopped almonds (optional)
2 teaspoons lemon juice
Dash pepper

Directions:
Place chicken pieces in shallow baking pan. Mix remaining ingredients and pour evenly over chicken. Bake uncovered for 1 hour at 325°F, basting occasionally.

Spicy Maple Wings

(Courtesy of the New York State Maple Producers Association,
www.nysmaple.com)

Ingredients:

2 pounds chicken wings
¼ cup pure maple syrup
2 tablespoons orange marmalade
2 tablespoons chili sauce
1 tablespoon poultry seasoning
Crushed red pepper (optional)
Salt and pepper to taste

Directions:

Preheat oven to 375°F. Place wings on non-stick baking sheet
and season with salt and pepper. Cover with foil and bake for 30
minutes. In a mixing bowl, whisk together maple syrup, orange
marmalade, chili sauce, and poultry seasoning. Add crushed red
pepper (if desired) for more heat in the sauce. Remove chicken
from oven, change temperature to broil. Remove the foil and
pour sauce over the wings, turning to coat well. Place back into
oven and broil for 7 minutes or until the wings are beginning to
crisp. Be careful not to overcook or scorch.

Chicken Teriyaki Maple Stir Fry

(Courtesy of the New York State Maple Producers Association,
www.nysmaple.com)

Ingredients:

4 teaspoons canola oil
1 tablespoon fresh minced garlic
1 pound boneless chicken breasts, cut into bite-sized strips
¼ cup teriyaki sauce
1 cup red pepper, cut into bite-sized strips
2 cups zucchini, cut into bite-sized strips

2 cups sliced mushrooms
1 cup snow peas
1 tablespoon soy sauce
1½ tablespoons pure maple cream
1–2 dashes hot sauce to taste (optional)

Directions:

Heat oil in wok until hot. Add fresh minced garlic and sauté until golden (1-2 minutes). Add chicken strips. Toss while cooking. After chicken is partially cooked (about 4 minutes) add teriyaki sauce and continue to toss to blend. Cook chicken until done. Remove chicken from pan with a slotted spoon. Set aside. Add red pepper strips and toss with spoon while cooking for about 1 minute. Continue to add vegetables in order listed, letting each addition heat and cook before adding the next (about a minute or so). Sprinkle soy sauce over vegetables and add a little more teriyaki sauce if needed. When vegetables are the desired doneness, add maple cream and toss to coat hot vegetables. Return chicken to pan and toss together with the vegetables until chicken is hot. If needed, add a little additional teriyaki sauce and hot sauce, if using. Serve over rice.

Pan-Seared Chicken Breast with Soy Maple Glaze

(Courtesy of the New York State Maple Producers Association, www.nysmaple.com)

Ingredients:

4 boneless skinless chicken breasts
2 cups pure maple syrup
¼ cup light soy sauce
1 cup water
¼ cup pure granulated maple sugar
2-inch piece fresh ginger, sliced
3 whole cloves garlic
4 whole star anise
2 tablespoons whole coriander

Directions:

Add all ingredients (except chicken) to sauce pan and simmer 20 minutes. Strain through fine mesh sieve. Pan sear four boneless chicken breasts (or a 1½-pound pork tenderloin or 24 large sea scallops). Preheat oven to 325°F. Place seared breasts in shallow baking pan and pour glaze on top, basting every five minutes; bake uncovered 15 minutes or until done. Serve with fresh roasted Brussels sprouts and steamed basmati rice or couscous.

Note: As an alternative, try reducing the strained glaze by half and use it as a sauce to drizzle over grilled salmon or boneless pork chops.

Maple Crunch Chicken

(Courtesy of the New York State Maple Producers Association,
www.nysmaple.com)

Ingredients:

½ cup margarine
1 cup instant oatmeal
¼ teaspoon salt
2 eggs
¼ cup pure maple syrup
1 fryer chicken, cut into pieces

Directions:

Melt margarine in a pan in 350°F oven. Mix together oatmeal and salt. Beat eggs with maple syrup. Dip chicken pieces into the egg mixture and then into oatmeal. Place chicken in pan with margarine and bake until tender, turning 2-3 times.

Orange Maple Glazed Wings

(Courtesy of the Massachusetts Maple Producers Association,
www.massmaple.org)

Ingredients:

1½ cups buttermilk
⅓ cup pure maple syrup
2 oranges, seeded, peeled, and sectioned
1 teaspoon cinnamon
20 chicken wings

Directions:

Process first four ingredients to make a coarse puree. Put wings
and puree in a gallon-sized bag and refrigerate for at least 2
hours, turning occasionally. Grill and baste with marinade until
done, avoid scorching.

Broiled Sirloin with Spicy Mustard and Apple Chutney

(Courtesy of NHLBI, part of NIH and HHS)

Ingredients:

Chutney:

1 Granny Smith apple, rinsed, peeled, cored, and diced (about 1 cup)

2 tablespoons shallots, minced

1 tablespoon garlic, minced (about 2–3 cloves)

½ cup canned no-salt-added diced tomatoes

2 ounces golden seedless raisins (about ½ cup)

¼ cup apple cider vinegar

2 tablespoons pure maple syrup

Steak:

4 (3 oz.) beef top sirloin steaks, lean

¼ teaspoon salt

¼ teaspoon ground black pepper

1 tablespoon olive oil

Mustard Dressing:

2 cups low-sodium beef broth

2 tablespoons Dijon mustard

2 tablespoons cornstarch

Directions:

Chutney:

Combine all the ingredients in a small saucepan. Bring to a boil over high heat, and simmer for 20 minutes or until apples are cooked and soft. Remove from the heat and hold warm, or cool and store.

Steak:

Preheat grill pan or oven broiler (with the rack 3 inches from heat source) on high temperature. Season the steaks with salt and pepper, and lightly coat with oil. Grill or broil 3–4 minutes on each side, or to your desired doneness (to a minimum internal temperature of 145ºF). Remove from the heat and set aside for 5 minutes.

Mustard Dressing:

Mix together beef broth, Dijon mustard, and cornstarch in a small saucepan. Bring to a boil on medium-high heat while stirring constantly. Lower the heat, and simmer for 2–3 minutes.

Serve each steak with ¼ cup of chutney and ½ cup of mustard dressing.

Maple Thyme Marinated Hanger Steak

(Courtesy of the New York State Maple Producers Association,
www.nysmaple.com)

Ingredients:

½ cup pure maple syrup
2 shallots, peeled and sliced
1 ounce fresh thyme
½ cup water
1 tablespoon kosher salt
1 teaspoon ground black pepper
2 pounds hanger steak

Directions:

Combine maple syrup, shallots, thyme, water, salt, and pepper
and place in medium-sized flat container. Add hanger steak and
marinate for 24 hours. Grill until desired temperature and doneness.

Maple Baked Ham

(Courtesy of Shaver-Hill Farm, www.shaverhillfarm.com)

Ingredients:

2 teaspoons dry mustard
2 teaspoons lemon juice
¾ cup pure maple syrup
6–8 thick ham slices

Directions:

Mix mustard and lemon juice, and stir until smooth. Add maple syrup and pour over ham slices in baking pan. Bake uncovered at 350°F for 50 minutes, basting every 10 minutes.

Spicy Maple Glazed Pork Chops

(Courtesy of the New York State Maple Producers Association,
www.nysmaple.com)

Ingredients:

1½ cups pure maple syrup
½ cup white vinegar
¼ cup horseradish
2 tablespoons ancho chile powder
4–8 pork chops

Directions:

Preheat oven to 400°F. Mix maple syrup, vinegar, horseradish
and chile powder well. Sear the pork chops on both sides, then
place in a baking dish. Set aside half of the glaze. Baste the
glaze over the chops and continue basting while the chops
finish cooking. Pour the reserved glaze over the chops just
before serving.

Braised Corned Beef with Maple

(Courtesy of the Massachusetts Maple Producers Association,
www.massmaple.org)

Ingredients:

4 pounds premium corned beef, desalted
1 cup pure maple syrup
¼ cup bourbon (optional)

Directions:

Place desalted brisket on rack in roasting pan and bake uncovered at 325°F for 30 minutes. Reduce heat to 275°F, cover, and bake 2 hours. Uncover, discard all but ½ cup liquid, add maple and bourbon (if using), and continue baking and basting frequently for an additional hour. Save liquid as table sauce.

Bacon Wrapped Scallops with Mango Maple Glaze

(Courtesy of the New York State Maple Producers Association,
www.nysmaple.com)

Ingredients:

8 scallops
4 strips bacon
½ cup pure maple syrup
1 cup mango sauce

Directions:

Preheat oven to 400°F. Wrap each scallop with ½ strip of bacon.
Place in a small baking dish. Mix the maple syrup and mango
sauce well. Baste and bake the scallops for 20 minutes until
nearly cooked. Baste again and then place under broiler for an
additional 10 minutes or until bacon begins to crisp.

Maple Broiled Scallops or Chicken Breast

(Courtesy of the Massachusetts Maple Producers Association, www.massmaple.org)

Ingredients:

¼ cup pure maple syrup
¼ teaspoon horseradish
4-6 sea scallops per person, or 1-inch pieces chicken breast
⅓ strip bacon, 1 per scallop or chicken piece

Directions:

Mix syrup and horseradish. Wrap each scallop or chicken piece with ⅓ strip bacon and secure with a toothpick. Place on broiler pan, brush with syrup, and broil 3 minutes. Turn, brush, and broil 2-3 minutes more, until bacon is crisp. Serve hot.

Maple Mustard Salmon

(Courtesy of the Massachusetts Maple Producers Association,
www.massmaple.org)

Ingredients:

4 salmon fillets
⅔ cup melted butter
½ tablespoon dried dill
½ cup pure maple syrup
¼ cup Dijon mustard

Directions:

Blend all ingredients (except salmon) over low heat until melted together. Grill or broil salmon, basting and turning until flaky and fully cooked.

Side Dishes
& Snacks

Baked Beans with Maple and Rum

(Courtesy of the Massachusetts Maple Producers Association,
www.massmaple.org)

Ingredients:

4 cups dry navy beans
3 quarts water
1 teaspoon baking soda
1 pound salt pork or ham
1 large onion
1 teaspoon dry mustard
1 cup pure maple syrup
1 tablespoon salt
4 apples, cored and unpeeled
1 cup pure maple sugar
½ cup butter
½ cup dark rum

Directions:

Rinse beans, cover with cold water, and soak overnight. Pour beans and water into large pot. Add baking soda and more water to cover beans. Bring to a boil uncovered and boil until some of the skins fall off when you blow on them. Line a bean pot with thin slices of the pork or ham, pour in beans and water. Roll onion in dry mustard until covered completely and bury it in the middle of the beans. Pour maple syrup and salt over top. Bake at 325°F for 4 to 5 hours. At the start of the last hour, place whole apples on top as close together as possible. Cream maple sugar and butter together and spread over top of apples. Pour rum over top just before serving.

Prairie Beans

(Courtesy of Chef Nancy Berkoff, R.D., "Vegetarian Journal",
The Vegetarian Resource Group, www.vrg.org)

Ingredients:

1 cup dried pinto beans
Water, to cover
2 tablespoons diced onions
½ cup chopped fresh tomatoes
½ cup diced canned tomatoes with liquid
½ cup diced fresh or canned chilies
2 tablespoons pure maple syrup
2 teaspoons chili powder
½ teaspoon dry mustard
1 teaspoon ground cumin
1 teaspoon dried oregano
2 teaspoons chopped fresh parsley

This type of dish was
a staple of American
pioneers and settlers.

Directions:

Rinse pinto beans with cold water. Place in a bowl, cover with
cold water, and allow to soak for at least 8 hours. Drain beans
and place in a large pot. Cover with water and bring to a fast
boil. Reduce heat, and allow beans to simmer until tender, about
50-60 minutes. Drain beans and save the cooking liquid. Place
beans in a refrigerator and allow to cool. Preheat oven to 350°F.
In a small bowl, combine half the cooking liquid (about 1 cup)
with onions, tomatoes, chilies, maple syrup, chili powder, mustard, cumin, oregano, and parsley. Mix into the cooling beans.
Pour bean mixture into a baking dish. Cover and bake for 1
hour or until bubbly.

Maple Glazed Vegetables

(Courtesy of Shaver-Hill Farm, www.shaverhillfarm.com)

Ingredients:

1 winter squash
1 sweet potato
3 carrots
Pure maple syrup, to cover

Directions:

Wash winter squash, sweet potato, and carrots. Slice lengthwise. Boil or steam until fork tender. Drain and place in shallow skillet. Pour on enough maple syrup to cover bottom of pan. Thin syrup by adding a small amount of water. Stir. Dot veggies with butter and cook uncovered in 300°F oven, or on top of stove at medium heat until glazed. Baste every 5 minutes.

Maple Baked Pears

(Courtesy of the New York State Maple Producers Association,
www.nysmaple.com)

Ingredients:

2 ripe but firm Bartlett pears
4 tablespoons lemon juice
1 tablespoon unsalted butter
2 tablespoons pure granulated maple sugar
2 tablespoons pure maple syrup (or more to taste)
½ teaspoon pure vanilla extract
Water (optional)

Directions:

Preheat oven to 375°F. Peel the pears and cut them in half
lengthwise. Using a melon baller or a spoon, scoop out the cores.
Brush the pears with lemon juice to prevent browning. Melt
the butter in an oven proof skillet just large enough to hold the
pears in a single layer. Add the granulated maple sugar and
cook over moderately low heat, stirring, until the sugar is dis-
solved. Add the pears and turn them several times to coat with
the syrup. Arrange the pears, cut side down, in a single layer
and bake for about 30 minutes, basting occasionally with pan
juices, until just softened and golden. Transfer the pears to a
platter and keep warm. If necessary, add a little water to the
skillet to thin the syrup. Remove from the heat and stir in the
vanilla. Pour the syrup over the pears and serve warm or at
room temperature.

Mini Maple Crab Cakes

(Courtesy of the New York State Maple Producers Association,
www.nysmaple.com)

Ingredients:

1 (16 oz.) can crabmeat,
squeezed dry
½ cup pure maple syrup
1 tablespoon Dijon or whole
grain mustard
1½ teaspoons Old Bay®
seasoning
1 teaspoon cajun seasoning
½ green bell pepper,
finely diced
½ red bell pepper, finely diced
1 tablespoon finely minced
shallots
2 eggs
½ lime, juiced
½ lime, zested

1½ cups Panko breadcrumbs
1¼ teaspoons salt
½ teaspoon black pepper
½ teaspoons Tabasco sauce
Oil, as needed
Panko breadcrumbs, as needed

Maple Cream Sauce:

½ cup sour cream
1 tablespoon pure maple cream
½ teaspoon lime juice
¼ teaspoon lime zest
¼ teaspoon Tabasco sauce
Salt and pepper to taste

Directions:

Combine all ingredients in a large bowl. Mix well. Let mixture
sit and absorb moisture for about 5 minutes. Form into mini pat-
ties. When ready to cook, heat a large sauté pan over high heat
until hot. Add enough oil to slightly coat the bottom of the pan.
Dredge each mini crab cake in more panko breadcrumbs. Cook
each crab cake over medium to medium-high heat until golden,
flip once, and cook until golden. Place crab cakes on a sheet tray
and finish baking in a 450°F oven until the internal temperature
reaches 165°F.

Maple Cream Sauce:

Whisk together sauce ingredients in a small bowl. Let sit 10
minutes to meld flavors. Place a small dollop on top of each crab
cake and serve.

Maple Baked Beans

(Courtesy of the New York State Maple Producers Association,
www.nysmaple.com)

Ingredients:

¾ cup pure granulated maple sugar
1 cup pure extra dark maple syrup
2 (40 oz.) cans Northern white beans
2 teaspoons prepared mustard
½ pound bacon, for garnish
Salt and pepper to taste

Directions:

Combine all ingredients (except bacon) in a mixing bowl, and
mix thoroughly. Place bean mixture in baking dish or pan. Place
strips of bacon on top of beans. Bake for 1 hour at 350°F.

Maple Glazed Carrots

(Courtesy of the New York State Maple Producers Association,
www.nysmaple.com)

Ingredients:

6 medium carrots
3 tablespoons butter
3 tablespoons pure maple syrup
½ teaspoon ginger
1 tablespoon pure granulated maple sugar

Directions:

Clean, wash, and slice carrots, then steam in a covered pan until tender. Melt butter. Add maple syrup and ginger to melted butter. Simmer carrots in this mixture until glazed. Sprinkle with granulated maple sugar before serving.

Maple Candied Sweet Potatoes

(Courtesy of Shaver-Hill Farm, www.shaverhillfarm.com)

Ingredients:

6 medium sweet potatoes
1 cup apple cider
1 teaspoon salt
1 tablespoon butter
½ cup pure maple syrup
½ cup water

Directions:

Boil unpeeled potatoes until nearly tender. Peel and slice into baking dish. Heat remaining ingredients to boiling. Pour over potatoes and bake at 300°F for 1 hour.

Maple Grilled Grapefruit

(Courtesy of the Massachusetts Maple Producers Association, www.massmaple.org)

Ingredients:

½ cup pure maple syrup
4 tablespoons melted butter
Dash cinnamon
2 grapefruit, cut in half
Handful golden raisins

Directions:

Combine syrup, butter, and cinnamon, and spread over the cut half of each grapefruit. Sprinkle raisins on top. Place on broiler pan about 4 inches below flame and broil 2-4 minutes. Serve hot.

Note: You may want to cut free each grapefruit section before broiling.

Maple-Glazed Butternut Squash

(Courtesy of the Massachusetts Maple Producers Association,
www.massmaple.org)

Ingredients:

1 medium butternut squash, peeled, seeded, cut into ½–inch slices
4 tablespoons pure maple syrup
¼ teaspoon ground mace
4 tablespoons dark rum
⅔ cup water

Directions:

Place all ingredients in a large saucepan. Bring to a boil, then simmer for 15 minutes, or until the squash is tender. Reserving the cooking liquid, transfer the squash with a slotted spoon to a heated serving dish. Boil the cooking liquid until it is thickened, then pour it over the squash.

Maple Fruit Punch

(Courtesy of Shaver-Hill Farm, www.shaverhillfarm.com)

Ingredients:

2 cups pure maple syrup
2 cups strawberry pieces (or other fruit)
1 cup orange juice
¾ cup crushed pineapple
2 cups strong tea
½ cup lemon juice

Directions:

Mix ingredients and chill for 1 hour. Add water or soda water to make one gallon of punch.

Maple Milk Punch

(Courtesy of Shaver-Hill Farm, www.shaverhillfarm.com)

Ingredients:

1 gallon milk
½ gallon vanilla ice cream
1 large bottle ginger ale
1 quart pure maple syrup

Directions:

Mix well and serve.

Hot Maple Apple Cider

(Courtesy of the Massachusetts Maple Producers Association, www.massmaple.org)

Ingredients:

6 cups apple cider
¼ cup pure maple syrup
1 orange peel, cut into strips
1 lemon peel, cut into strips
2 cinnamon sticks
6 whole cloves
6 whole allspice berries
Spice bag
String

Directions:

Pour cider and syrup into large pot. Place peels and spices in center of a spice bag and tie with a piece of string. Drop spice bundle into liquid and heat over medium heat for about 10 minutes. Remove spice bag and discard. Ladle maple cider into mugs and serve warm.

Optional: Garnish with a stick of cinnamon for stirring, and top with whipped cream or a thin slice of lemon or orange.

Maple Milkshake

(Courtesy of the New York State Maple Producers Association,
www.nysmaple.com)

Ingredients:

2 scoops vanilla ice cream
1 cup milk
½ cup pure maple syrup

Directions:

Place ingredients in blender and blend until well mixed, or
shake all ingredients thoroughly in a tightly covered container.

Desserts

Maple Bavarian Cream

Ingredients:

4 egg yolks
1 cup pure maple syrup
1 package gelatin
2 tablespoons cold water
4 egg whites
½ pint cream
Pinch salt

Directions:

Boil egg yolks, maple syrup, and salt in a double boiler until it reaches the consistency of custard. Stir while cooking. Soak gelatin in the water. Add to the maple syrup mixture while still hot. Let cool. Beat the egg whites until stiff and combine with the mixture. Add the cream. Place in a mold to cool.

Molasses Candy

Ingredients:

1 cup molasses
1 tablespoon vinegar
1 tablespoon butter
½ cup pure maple syrup
½ cup white sugar

Directions:

Boil all ingredients together until brittle when dropped in water.
Pull when cool enough to handle.

Maple Macadamia Nut Parfait

(Courtesy of the New York State Maple Producers Association,
www.nysmaple.com)

Ingredients:

1 package Knox® gelatine
1 cup cold water
1 cup pure maple syrup
Macadamia nuts or other available nuts

Directions:

Soak gelatine in ¼ cup cold water for 5 minutes. Bring syrup
to boil. Stir in gelatine and stir until clear. Add remaining cold
water. Stir. Refrigerate. When mixture is almost set, beat until
fluffy. Put in glasses, then into refrigerator. When serving, deco-
rate with whipped cream, nuts, or cherries as desired.

Serves 4.

Almond Rice Pudding

(Courtesy of Chef Nancy Berkoff, R.D., "Vegan Meals for One or
Two", The Vegetarian Resource Group, www.vrg.org)

Ingredients:

½ cup uncooked white and brown rice
1 cup water
2 cups almond milk (or soy or rice milk with 1 tablespoon
almond extract)
¼ cup pure maple syrup
½ teaspoon vanilla extract
1 teaspoon cinnamon
¼ cup raisins, dried cranberries, or dried blueberries

Directions:

In a medium-sized saucepan, combine rice and water. Bring to a
fast boil, cover, and reduce heat. Simmer for 15 minutes or until
all the water is absorbed. Stir in almond milk, maple syrup,
and vanilla, stirring until the rice mixture is as thick as soupy
cooked cereal (this should take approximately 30 minutes).
Remove from heat and stir in cinnamon and raisin or other
dried fruit. Eat warm or refrigerate until you're ready to eat.

Note: Pudding, if overcooked, will become dry instead of creamy.

Couscous Pudding
(Courtesy of Debra Wasserman, "Conveniently Vegan", The
Vegetarian Resource Group, www.vrg.org)

Ingredients:
1½ cups water
5 ounces couscous (a little less than 1 cup)
½ cup dried fruit (such as raisins, chopped figs or dates)
1½ cups soymilk or other milk alternative
¼ cup pure maple syrup
¼ teaspoon cinnamon
2 tablespoons cornstarch

Directions:
Bring water to a boil in a small pot. Add couscous and dried
fruit. Cover pot, remove from heat, and allow to sit 5 minutes.
Meanwhile, in a separate medium-sized pot, heat remaining
ingredients over medium-high heat until the pudding starts
to thicken (about 3 minutes). While heating, stir often with a
whisk. Once pudding thickens, remove from heat and add cooked
couscous mixture. Mix well. Pour pudding into a serving dish
and chill for at least 1 hour before serving.

Note: Experiment with different types of dried fruit for variety.

Maple Apple Squares

(Courtesy of the New York State Maple Producers Association,
www.nysmaple.com)

Ingredients:

1 box yellow cake mix
1 stick butter
¼ cup pure maple syrup
3-4 apples
1 (8 oz.) package sour cream
1 egg
¼ pure granulated maple sugar
1 teaspoon cinnamon
Whipped cream

Directions:

In bowl, place yellow cake mix and butter (or margarine or butter substitute). Mix together with pastry blender until crumbly and reserve ⅔ cup in separate bowl. Pat the mixture into a 9 x 13-inch pan and top with thinly sliced apples. Mix together sour cream and egg, then spread over apples. Add maple sugar and cinnamon to the reserved ⅔ cup mixture and spread over the top of the sour cream layer. Bake at 350°F for 25 to 30 minutes. When cool, cut into squares and drizzle with maple syrup and a dollop of whipped cream.

Maple Lava Cakes

(Courtesy of the New York State Maple Producers Association,
www.nysmaple.com)

Ingredients:

1½ cups sugar
½ cup butter
¼ cup pure maple syrup
2 eggs
½ cup milk
1¾ cups flour
½ teaspoon baking powder
¾ cup pure maple cream

Directions:

Preheat oven to 400°F. Butter 8 ramekins (medium custard
cups). Beat together sugar and butter, then add the maple syrup.
Add eggs one at a time. Add milk and mix well. In a separate
bowl, mix the flour and baking powder, then add to batter and
mix until smooth. Pour batter into the ramekins (about 6-7
tablespoons per cup). Put the ramekins on a cookie sheet and
place in oven. Bake about 20 minutes or until the edges start to
pull away. The centers will still be soft. Loosen the sides with a
knife and turn upside down onto a dessert plate that smeared
with maple cream. Remove the ramekin. Finish with maple
cream on the top of each cake and enjoy.

Maple Cheesecake
(Courtesy of Shaver-Hill Farm, www.shaverhillfarm.com)

Ingredients:
1½ cups graham cracker crumbs
6 tablespoons sugar
⅓ cup melted butter or margarine
¾ cup pure maple syrup
¼ cup heavy cream
1½ pounds cream cheese, softened
3 eggs
1½ teaspoons vanilla
1½ cups sour cream

Directions:
Combine graham cracker crumbs, 2 tablespoons of sugar, and melted butter or margarine in a small mixing bowl and then press into the bottom of a 9-inch springform pan and freeze. Bring the maple syrup to a boil over medium heat in a saucepan. Boil three minutes, then remove from heat and stir in the heavy cream. Scrape into a bowl and refrigerate. Using an electric mixer, beat the cream cheese until light and fluffy. Add the remaining 4 tablespoons of sugar and beat briefly, then add the eggs. When the maple syrup is no longer warm to the touch, gradually beat it in, followed by the vanilla and sour cream. Spread the filling mixture into the chilled pan and bake for 1 hour. Transfer to a rack and thoroughly cool. Cover and chill at least 6 hours before serving.

Rolled Maple Sugar Cookies

(Courtesy of the New York State Maple Producers Association,
www.nysmaple.com)

Ingredients:

1 cup shortening
¾ cup pure maple sugar
1 cup white sugar
2 eggs, well beaten
2 tablespoons milk
2 teaspoons vanilla
4 cups flour
2 teaspoons baking powder
½ teaspoon salt

Directions:

Cream shortening with sugars. Add well-beaten eggs, milk and vanilla. Add flour, baking powder, and salt, sifted together. Mix and chill thoroughly. Roll out thin on floured board and cut with cookie cutter. Bake on greased cookie sheets in 350°F oven for 10 minutes.

Makes 6 dozen 3-inch cookies.

Maple Oatmeal Cookies
(Courtesy of Shaver-Hill Farm, www.shaverhillfarm.com)

Ingredients:

1½ cups butter
1¾ cups pure maple syrup
1 cup granulated sugar
2 eggs
2 teaspoons vanilla
6 cups oats, uncooked
2 cups all-purpose flour
1 teaspoon salt
2 teaspoons baking soda

Directions:

Preheat oven to 350°F. Beat together butter, syrup, sugar, eggs and vanilla. Add oats. Mix together and add flour, salt and baking soda. Mix well. Drop by rounded teaspoonfuls onto greased cookie sheet. Bake for 12 to 15 minutes.

Note: For variety, add ½ cup of any or all of the following: chopped nuts, raisins, chocolate chips or coconut.

Sliced Maple-Peanut Butter Cookies

(Courtesy of Shaver-Hill Farm, www.shaverhillfarm.com)

Ingredients:

½ cup crunchy style peanut butter
½ cup shortening, softened
½ cup light brown sugar
½ cup pure maple syrup
1 egg, beaten
2 cups unsifted flour
½ teaspoon baking powder
½ teaspoon baking soda
½ teaspoon salt

Directions:

Blend together the peanut butter and shortening, then beat in the brown sugar and maple syrup. Add egg, beat well. Sift flour with the baking powder, baking soda, and salt. Add to first mixture, beating thoroughly. Turn out on floured board and divide in half. Shape each half into a roll about 2-inches in diameter. Wrap well in waxed paper and chill overnight. Cut in ¼-inch slices. Bake on ungreased cookie sheet in 350°F oven for about 12 minutes or until brown.

Makes about 4 dozen.

Maple Nut Fudge

(Courtesy of the Massachusetts Maple Producers Association,
www.massmaple.org)

Ingredients:

2 cups sugar
1 cup pure maple syrup
2 tablespoons corn syrup
½ cup milk
1 teaspoon vanilla
1 cup chopped nuts
1 tablespoon butter

Directions:

Boil sugar, maple syrup, corn syrup, and milk, stirring constantly until 238°F. Remove from heat. Cool to 110°F. Add vanilla, nuts, and butter. Beat until thick and creamy. Pour into 8-inch pan and cut into squares when chilled.

Maple Cream Cheese Icing

(Courtesy of the New York State Maple Producers Association,
www.nysmaple.com)

Ingredients:

10 ounces cream cheese, room temperature
5 tablespoons butter, room temperature
2½ cups confectioner's sugar
¼ cup pure maple syrup

Directions:

Beat cream cheese and butter until light and fluffy. Add confectioner's sugar and beat until well blended. Add in maple syrup. Chill until just firm enough to spread.

Maple Walnut Cream Cake

Ingredients:

⅓ cup butter
¾ cup sugar
1½ cups flour
2½ teaspoons baking powder
½ cup milk
1 teaspoon vanilla
2 egg whites

Directions:

Cream the butter and sugar. Mix and sift the flour with the baking powder, then add to the milk and vanilla. Beat thoroughly. Fold in egg whites, beaten stiff. Bake in round shallow pans, lined and buttered. When cool, trim, fill with maple frosting (see page 68), and sprinkle ½ cup small pieces of walnut over bottom cake. Place second cake on top and cover top and sides with maple frosting.

Maple Frosting

Ingredients:

1 cup pure maple syrup
2 egg whites, beaten stiff

Directions:

Boil maple syrup until it threads. Slowly pour into the egg whites. Beat constantly until frosting becomes thick enough to spread.

Maple Sugar Kisses

(Courtesy of the New York State Maple Producers Association,
www.nysmaple.com)

Ingredients:

1 cup pure maple sugar
½ cup brown sugar
½ cup water
¼ teaspoon cream of tartar
6 marshmallows
1 egg white

Directions:

Boil sugars, water, and cream of tartar in saucepan until mixture becomes brittle when dropped in cold water. Cut marshmallows into small pieces and add to mixture. Let stand 5 minutes until melted. Pour over stiffly beaten egg white. Beat until light. Drop from teaspoon onto wax paper. Garnish with candied cherry or pecan halves. Makes 30 kisses.

Maple Date Ball Cookies

(Courtesy of the New York State Maple Producers Association,
www.nysmaple.com)

Ingredients:

1 cup pure granulated maple sugar
1 cup dates, finely chopped
1 stick butter
1½ cups Rice Krispies®
Flaked coconut
1 cup chopped nuts and/or ½ cup wheat germ (optional)

Directions:

In 3-quart saucepan combine maple sugar, dates, and butter.
Cook, stirring constantly, until butter and sugar melt (about 4
to 5 minutes). Remove from heat and add Rice Krispies® (if not
using nuts, you can add more Rice Krispies®). Stir until well
blended. Put coconut in small bowl. With small cookie scoop,
scoop date mixture and drop into coconut. Putting some coconut
in your hands, roll the cookies and put into a container that can
be tightly sealed (add a bit of coconut to the bottom of the container first to prevent sticking). When all the cookies are in the
container, sprinkle with a bit more coconut. Seal tightly. These
can be stored in the refrigerator for up to 2 weeks.

Maple Bread Pudding

(Courtesy of the Massachusetts Maple Producers Association,
www.massmaple.org)

Ingredients:

¾ cup pure maple syrup
3 slices bread, crusts removed
1 tablespoon butter
½ cup nutmeats or raisins
1 teaspoon lemon juice
2 eggs
2 cups milk
¼ teaspoon salt
¼ teaspoon vanilla

Directions:

Pour maple syrup into a double boiler. Butter each slice of bread
and cube. Add to syrup. Add nuts or raisins and lemon juice.
Beat together eggs, milk, salt, and vanilla, then pour over bread
mixture. Do not stir. Set over gently boiling water. Cook for 1
hour to make a sauce. Spoon it over each serving.

Blueberry Maple Mousse

(Courtesy of the Massachusetts Maple Producers Association,
www.massmaple.org)

Ingredients:

6 egg yolks
¾ cup pure maple syrup, heated
1 pint heavy cream
1 pint blueberries

Directions:

Beat yolks in bowl or top of a double boiler until thick. Beat in hot syrup. Put over simmering water and cook, beating constantly until slightly thickened. Cool. Beat cream until it forms stiff peaks and fold into the yolk mixture. Fold in half of the blueberries. Pour into a 1½ quart mold. Freeze overnight. Before serving, garnish with remainder of berries.

Serves 8-10.

Maple Bars

(Courtesy of the Massachusetts Maple Producers Association,
www.massmaple.org)

Ingredients:

½ cup sugar
⅔ cup sifted flour
½ cup soft shortening (¼ cup butter and ¼ cup shortening)
1 cup nutmeats
1 cup rolled oats
½ teaspoon baking powder
½ cup pure maple syrup
1 teaspoon vanilla
1 egg

Directions:

Heat oven to 350°F. Grease a square pan, 8 x 8-inches. Mix all
ingredients thoroughly. Spread in prepared pan. Bake 30-35
minutes. Cut into squares while still warm.

Maple Walnut Cream Pie

(Courtesy of the Massachusetts Maple Producers Association,
www.massmaple.org)

Ingredients:

2 cups milk
2 cups pure maple syrup
3 egg yolks, well-beaten
6 tablespoons flour
1 teaspoon vanilla
½ cup chopped walnuts
½ cup yogurt or whipped cream
Dash salt

Directions:

Combine milk, syrup, egg yolks, and flour in double boiler. Cook slowly over simmering water for about 30 minutes. Add dash of salt and vanilla. Pour in baked pie shell. Sprinkle with half the nuts. Chill. Shortly before serving, spread yogurt or whipped cream and sprinkle the rest of the nuts.

Breads

Cornbread

(Courtesy of Debra Wasserman and Reed Mangels, Ph.D., R.D., "Simply Vegan", The Vegetarian Resource Group, www.vrg.org)

Ingredients:

1 cup cornmeal
1 cup whole wheat flour
1 tablespoon baking powder
¼ cup oil
1 cup soy milk
⅓ cup molasses or pure maple syrup

Directions:

Preheat oven to 375°F. Mix ingredients together in bowl. Pour batter into lightly oiled 8-inch round pan. Bake for 20 minutes.

Variation: Prepare same batter, and pour into lightly oiled muffin tins. Bake at the same temperature for the same amount of time. Children will especially enjoy these muffins.

Maple-Lemon Zucchini Bread

(Courtesy of the New York State Maple Producers Association,
www.nysmaple.com)

Ingredients:

3 eggs
1 cup pure maple syrup
½ cup vegetable oil
1 teaspoon vanilla extract
Zest of 1 lemon, finely grated
1½ cups grated zucchini
1½ cups unbleached or all-purpose flour
1 cup whole wheat flour
1 tablespoon baking powder
½ teaspoon salt

Directions:

Preheat oven to 350°F. Grease a 9 x 5-inch pan and set aside.
Beat the eggs with an electric mixer for 2 minutes. Gradually
add the maple syrup, oil, vanilla, and lemon zest. Stir in the zucchini. Combine the unbleached and wheat flours, baking powder,
and salt in a large bowl. Make a well in the center, then stir in
the zucchini mixture. Blend just until smooth, then turn into the
prepared pan. Bake for 50 to 60 minutes, until a tester inserted
into the center comes out clean. Cool in the pan for 5 to 10 minutes, then remove and cool completely on a wire rack.

Maple Monkey Bread

(Courtesy of the New York State Maple Producers Association,
www.nysmaple.com)

Ingredients:

2 (7½ oz.) packs refrigerated biscuits
½ cup butter, melted
½ cup pure granulated maple sugar mixed with 1 teaspoon cinnamon
½ cup chopped walnuts (optional)
½ cup pure maple syrup

Directions:

Preheat oven to 350°F. Spray 10-inch bundt pan with non-stick cooking spray. Cut biscuits into quarters. Dip in melted butter, then roll the dough in the maple/cinnamon sugar and put in bundt pan in layers. Sprinkle chopped nuts as you go, if desired. Combine remaining butter and maple syrup and pour over top. Bake for 25-30 minutes or until golden brown. Be careful not to overcook or scorch. Immediately invert onto plate and pull pieces apart to serve.

Maple Biscuits

(Courtesy of Shaver-Hill Farm, www.shaverhillfarm.com)

Ingredients:

2 cups all-purpose flour
¾ teaspoon salt
1 tablespoon baking powder
4 tablespoons cold butter
¾ cup heavy cream
¼ cup pure maple syrup
2 tablespoons butter, melted
2 tablespoons pure maple syrup

Directions:

Preheat oven to 425°F. Combine dry ingredients in mixing bowl. Cut the butter into the flour mixture until it resembles coarse meal. Blend the heavy cream and ¼ cup maple syrup and pour into a well in the flour mixture. Stir until a sticky dough forms. Turn the dough onto a lightly floured surface and gently knead 4 or 5 times. Pat or roll to a ¾-inch thickness. Cut into rounds with a biscuit cutter or glass and place on lightly greased baking sheet. Melt 2 tablespoons of butter and mix with 2 tablespoons of maple syrup, stirring to blend. Brush some of the maple syrup and butter mixture on each biscuit. Bake until golden, about 15 minutes. Serve hot.

Maple Apple Dumplings

(Courtesy of the New York State Maple Producers Association,
www.nysmaple.com)

Ingredients:

Pie pastry
4 medium apples
⅓ cup pure granulated maple sugar
½ teaspoon cinnamon
2 tablespoons butter or margarine
2 cups pure maple syrup

Directions:

Heat oven to 425°F. Roll out pastry and cut into 7-inch squares.
Pare and core one apple for each dumpling. Place apple in center
of each square. Mix together the maple sugar and cinnamon,
and fill apple cavities. Dot each apple top with about ½ teaspoon
butter. Bring opposite points of pastry up over the apple. Moist-
en pastry to seal it together. Place in baking dish. Bake for 40 to
45 minutes until crust is nicely browned and apples are cooked
through (test with fork). Put dumpling on serving dish. Drizzle
with hot maple syrup and top with whipped cream or ice cream.

Old-Time Maple Gingerbread

(Courtesy of the Massachusetts Maple Producers Association,
www.massmaple.org)

Ingredients:

2 cups flour
1 teaspoon ginger
½ teaspoon salt
1 teaspoon baking soda
1 cup pure maple syrup
1 egg, beaten
1 cup sour cream

Directions:

Combine and sift dry ingredients. Mix maple syrup with beaten
egg and add the sour cream. Combine the mixture and bake in
medium oven for about 40 minutes. Serve with warm maple
hard sauce or whipped cream.

Spreads & Sauces

Ginger-Teriyaki Sauce

(Courtesy of Chef Nancy Berkoff, R.D., "Vegetarian Journal",
The Vegetarian Resource Group, www.vrg.org)

Ingredients:

½ cup low-sodium soy sauce
4 teaspoons rice wine or
sherry
3 teaspoons sesame oil
2 tablespoons pure maple
syrup
2 cloves garlic, minced
1 tablespoon minced fresh ginger
2 tablespoons chopped fresh scallions

Use as a dipping sauce for steamed vegetables or to perk up steamed rice.

Directions:

Whisk all ingredients together until well combined. Pour into a glass or plastic container and refrigerate. It will last 5-7 days in the refrigerator.

Note: Regular soy sauce can be used, if desired.

This recipe does need wine or sherry for an authentic taste. If wine or sherry is not available, substitute 2 teaspoons orange juice concentrate and 1 teaspoon white vinegar. This will make an acceptable sauce.

Makes about 16 tablespoons.

Maple Fruit Dip

(Courtesy of the New York State Maple Producers Association, www.nysmaple.com)

Ingredients:

1 (8 oz.) package cream cheese, room temperature
½ cup sour cream
¼ cup pure granulated maple sugar
2 tablespoons pure maple syrup
Assorted fruits (such as peaches, pears, apples, grapes, pineapple, cantaloupe, strawberries, or kiwi)

Directions:

Fold all ingredients into the cream cheese. Serve atop assorted fruits.

Maple Mocha Topping

(Courtesy of the Massachusetts Maple Producers Association,
www.massmaple.org)

Ingredients:

2 egg whites, beaten until stiff
2 teaspoons instant coffee
½ teaspoon vanilla
¼ cup sugar
¾ cup pure maple syrup

Directions:

Beat until thickened. Serve over ice cream or angel cake.

Makes 2 cups.

Maple Jelly

(Courtesy of the Massachusetts Maple Producers Association,
www.massmaple.org)

Ingredients:

3 cups cold water
2 teaspoons Genugel® (pectin does not work with maple syrup)
½ gallon Grade A Medium Amber pure maple syrup

Directions:

Whisk the Genugel® into the cold water first, then add to syrup.
Make sure the pot is at least 3 times the size of the liquid, as
it foams up during boil. Boil all ingredients to 217.5°F. Some
people prefer to boil to 219°F, but that makes unnecessarily
hard jelly and wastes more content. The objective is to make
clear jelly. Any infusion of air through stirring or filling of the
jars will put air bubbles into the jelly. It will still taste fine, but
won't look as appealing. It helps greatly to keep a low flame
under the jelly while bottling, as it will gel really fast and heat
keeps it liquid longer.

First, skim off the surface foam as minimally as possible to
prevent waste. Then use a cup or ladle large enough to fill each
clean jar with one pour. Going back and adding more to fill the
jar will cause air bubbles and layering. Cap the filled jars and
process them in a hot water bath for 10 minutes at 180°F. Depending on how successful you are at skimming, a half gallon of
syrup will net you five to seven 8-oz. jars of maple jelly.

Note: Genugel® is available from maple syrup equipment suppli-
ers.

Easy Maple Butter

(Courtesy of the New York State Maple Producers Association,
www.nysmaple.com)

Ingredients:

½ cup butter, softened
¼ cup pure maple syrup

Directions:

In a food processor, whip butter until creamy. Gradually add the
maple syrup and whip until the mixture is smooth.

Note: This maple butter is delicious served on waffles or spread
on thin, rolled crepes.

Maple Butter

(Courtesy of the New York State Maple Producers Association,
www.nysmaple.com)

Ingredients:

1 cup butter, softened
1 teaspoon lemon rind, grated
½ teaspoon nutmeg
⅔ cup pure maple syrup

Directions:

In a bowl, combine butter, lemon rind, and nutmeg; beat until
light and fluffy. Add the syrup, ⅓ cup at a time, beating well
after each addition. Spoon into small crocks or jars. Cover with
lids or plastic wrap; refrigerate. Can be refrigerated for up to 3
weeks.

Makes 2 cups.

Maple Whipped Butter

(Courtesy of the New York State Maple Producers Association,
www.nysmaple.com)

Ingredients:

1 cup butter
1¼ cups pure maple syrup
¼ teaspoon plain gelatin
1 teaspoon cold water

Directions:

Whip butter in mixer until fluffy. Slowly drizzle maple syrup on butter. Soak gelatin in cold water, then dissolve over hot water. Cool slightly and slowly add to butter. Mix well.

Cinnamon Maple Butter

(Courtesy of the New York State Maple Producers Association,
www.nysmaple.com)

Ingredients:

1 pound unsalted butter, softened
2 tablespoons pure maple syrup
2 drops vanilla extract
¼ teaspoon cinnamon
⅛ teaspoon salt

Directions:

Combine all ingredients, mixing thoroughly. Pack into crock or
pottery dish. Refrigerate. Garnish with cinnamon stick when
serving.

Cranberry Maple Butter

(Courtesy of the New York State Maple Producers Association,
www.nysmaple.com)

Ingredients:

½ cup water
12 ounces cranberries, fresh or frozen
½ cup pure maple syrup
6 tablespoons brown sugar
½ teaspoon cinnamon
½ teaspoon vanilla

Directions:

Combine the water and cranberries in a large saucepan. Bring to a boil; cover, reduce heat and simmer for 5 minutes or until the berries pop. Process the cranberry mixture until smooth. Combine cranberry mixture with maple syrup, sugar, and cinnamon and bring to a boil. Reduce heat, and simmer, uncovered, for 25 minutes or until mixture is thick. Stir frequently. Stir in vanilla. Cool and store in the refrigerator up to 2 months.

Maple Nutmeg Butter

(Courtesy of the New York State Maple Producers Association,
www.nysmaple.com)

Ingredients:

1 stick unsalted butter, softened
2 tablespoons pure maple syrup
⅛ teaspoon ground nutmeg

Directions:

Place all ingredients in a medium bowl and whisk or blend
with a hand blender for a creamier texture, until light and well
blended.

Maple-Pecan Butter

(Courtesy of the New York State Maple Producers Association,
www.nysmaple.com)

Ingredients:

½ cup toasted pecans
½ cup unsalted butter, softened and chopped
2 tablespoons pure maple syrup

Directions:

In a food processor, pulse pecans until finely chopped. Remove. In processor, combine butter and maple syrup. Process until blended. Add pecans. Process by pulsing just until mixed. Roll butter mixture into a log shape on plastic wrap, using wrap to help form butter. Wrap and refrigerate at least 1 to 2 hours before serving in slices. Store in the refrigerator up to 2 weeks or freeze up to 1 month.

Spiced Maple Butter

(Courtesy of the New York State Maple Producers Association,
www.nysmaple.com)

Ingredients:

½ cup butter
½ teaspoon pumpkin pie spice
2 tablespoons pure maple syrup

Directions:

Beat in a small bowl until light and fluffy.

Maple Pepper Butter and Glaze

(Courtesy of the New York State Maple Producers Association,
www.nysmaple.com)

Ingredients:

2 sticks butter, softened
½ cup plus 2 tablespoons pure maple syrup
¼ cup lemon juice
2 teaspoons lemon zest, finely grated
1 tablespoon black pepper, coarsely ground
2 teaspoons coarse salt
½ teaspoon black pepper, finely ground

Directions:

In a food processor, combine the butter, 6 tablespoons maple
syrup, 3 tablespoons lemon juice, lemon zest, coarsely-ground
pepper, and salt. Process until blended and transfer to a bowl. In
another bowl, combine the remaining ¼ cup maple syrup,
1 tablespoon lemon juice, and the finely-ground pepper to make
glaze.

Maple Cream Cheese Spread

(Courtesy of the New York State Maple Producers Association,
www.nysmaple.com)

Ingredients:

½ cup pure maple cream
6 ounces cream cheese, softened

Directions:

In a food processor or with an electric mixer, whip the maple
cream and the cream cheese together until light and fluffy. The
spread can be refrigerated in a covered container, for up to 3
weeks.

Resources

Cornell Sugar Maple Research & Extension Program
maple.dnr.cornell.edu
The Cornell Sugar Maple Research & Extension Program offers a variety of maple syrup facts, teaching resources, research data, recipes, and links to helpful websites and publications.

Eat Well Guide
www.eatwellguide.org
The Eat Well Guide offers a comprehensive search of local organizations, farms, farmers markets, restaurants, and co-ops that offer local, organic, and sustainable food.

Local.com
www.local.com
Search for local fruit and vegetable stands, farms, organizations, and more on this website.

Local Harvest
www.localharvest.org
Use the search tool provided by the Local Harvest website to find farmers' markets, co-ops, farms, and other sustainable food sources in your local area.

Massachusetts Maple Producers Association
www.massmaple.org
Massachusetts Maple Producers Association is a non-profit organization dedicated to the preservation and promotion of maple sugaring in Massachusetts. Visit this website to learn more about the maple sugaring process, the nutritional benefits of maple syrup, or to learn about maple related events in or near Massachusetts. The site also offers recipes, links, and basic data about maple syrup and other products.

National Heart, Lung and Blood Institute (NHLBI)
www.nhlbi.nih.gov
Visit the website of the National Heart, Lung and Blood Institute (NHLBI) to find extensive research and information about healthy living and the prevention and treatment of heart, lung, and blood diseases. The site also provides healthy recipes and links to other helpful organizations.

New York State Maple Producers Association
www.nysmaple.com
The New York State Maple Producers Association is an organization consisting of almost 500 syrup makers in North America and supports the maple industry in New York State. Visit this website to find recipes, maple events, helpful data and links, or to learn about their educational programs for maple producers. Also, use the Find-a-Producer feature to locate maple producers throughout New York State.

Shaver-Hill Farm
www.shaverhillfarm.com
Shaver-Hill Farm is a family-owned maple producer nestled in the Catskills Mountains of New York State. Visit their website to learn more about their maple farm, the products they provide, or to find ideas for cooking with maple.

The Vegetarian Resource Group
www.vrg.org
Visit the website for the Vegetarian Resource Group (VRG) to learn more about vegetarianism, health, nutrition, ecology, ethics, and world hunger. The site offers a wealth of recipes, links, and nutritional information, and many other resources.

State and Regional Maple Producers Groups and Associations:

Maine Maple Producers Association
www.mainemapleproducers.com

Maple Syrup Producers Association of Connecticut
www.ctmaple.org

Massachusetts Maple Producers Association
www.massmaple.org

Michigan Maple Syrup Association
www.mi-maplesyrup.com

New Hampshire Maple Producers Association
www.nhmapleproducers.com

New York State Maple Association
www.nysmaple.com

North American Maple Syrup Council
northamericanmaple.org

Ohio Maple Producers Association
www.ohiomapleproducers.com

Vermont Maple Sugar Makers Association
vermontmaple.org

Wisconsin Maple Syrup Producers Association
www.wismaple.org